IMAGES
of America

CANTON
OHIO

This is Bezaleel Wells, the man who is credited with founding Canton. Mr. Wells purchased the land on which the city now sits sight unseen, as he had heard that land west of Salem was to be opened for settlement.

The name Canton has always been a source of conjecture. No one is certain whether he named the city for Canton, China, or for the name a friend of his had given his estate outside Baltimore, Maryland, or the name given to some Swiss counties. All we know for certain is that Canton has become a delightful place in which to live.

IT'S OVER!!! This was just about all that could be heard on V-J Day in 1945. The long nightmare that was World War II was finally over, with the unconditional surrender of Japan. The euphoria in Canton was overwhelming. The people just burst into the streets with shouts of joy. Everyone was your friend, there was nothing so important as the knowledge that your son, brother, husband, cousin, or nephew would soon be home to pick up life where it left off, after the attack on Pearl Harbor in December of 1941.

Life would never be the same in Canton—it just got better and better. That is why we celebrate our city in this book!

IMAGES
of America

CANTON
OHIO

Ronald E. Sterling
and the Canton Preservation Society

ARCADIA
PUBLISHING

Published by Arcadia Publishing
Charleston, South Carolina

Library of Congress Catalog Card Number: 2008921894

For all general information contact Arcadia Publishing at:
Telephone 843-853-2070
Fax 843-853-0044
E-mail sales@arcadiapublishing.com
For customer service and orders:
Toll-Free 1-888-313-2665

Visit us on the Internet at www.arcadiapublishing.com

The Daniel Worley, Canton's 1880s-era pumper, struts its stuff during one of the last exhibitions of nineteenth-century fire fighting in a Memorial Day parade. This antique piece is on display in the McKinley Museum of History, Science, and Industry in Canton.

CONTENTS

ACKNOWLEDGMENTS

When an author chooses to write a book, one thing is assured—that it would never get into print without the help of many people. I cannot begin to thank my employer, the Canton Preservation Society, for all the encouragement I have been given. The Board of Trustees have seen some of our projects fall behind schedule while this book took shape.

The Society has a very extensive photographic archive, and I did not know how extensive it was until a young lady from Kent State University's Stark Campus came to us as an intern. Ruth Hetrick has been a veritable dervish in digging out obscure photos which appear in this book.

Ruth Whitticar and Jane Noel, two of the trustees with such patience, provided some very rare photos—do not miss the Wyant and Noel Grocery Store and the pseudo-aerial photo of the Dueber Hampden Watch Works. Jane's grandfather was the Noel of the grocery, and Ruth's father, Eugene Miday, climbed up a smokestack in Waterworks Park to take the picture of Dueber Hampden. He also snapped the pictures of Mr. Timken's plane.

I apologize in advance for the limited number of ethnic groups in the book. It is not an intentional oversight, but is merely due to space constraints.

I am deeply indebted to the following people in our community for their help with this project. Marian Mazzarella, who introduced me to Dorothy and Florence DioGuardi, and who provided me with much of the textual material for the Italian section. To Omar and Rose Perez of Los Jubilados de la Colonia Espaniola (you were right, it does sound better than the Spanish-American Retirees Club), who provided such wonderful pictures of the Spanish fiestas. To Theresa Greene, for giving so freely of the photos of her late son Antonio, and her parents, the Alarcons. I am happy that this book will help commemorate Antonio's life.

To Joe Manolos and George Michalos, for helping to provide the photos of the moving of St. Haralambos, and to the Greek community, for holding on to your tradition at no small cost.

Ernest Cohen—you sir are a true community treasure, for being available to tell me about all the Jewish history in Canton. Adele Gelb, of the *Stark Jewish News*, and Rabbi John Spitzer, for pointing me in Ernie's direction. Elaine Garfinkle, who, as past editor of the *Stark Jewish News*, collected several oral histories of early Jewish citizens.

Joe Moeglin, for helping me acquire some of his mother, Genevieve's, school photos, and Winona Rossiter, for loaning me her school photos for copying. Both of these ladies are true pioneers at St. Peter's Roman Catholic Church. To Mary Margaret at St. John's, for her assistance in compiling the information about the history of the oldest parish in the city.

To Pete Fierle at the National Pro Football Hall of Fame, for the loan of the picture of Ralph Hay's Hupmbile/Jordan Dealership. I am greatly appreciative.

To the city of Canton, Ohio, thank you for providing William McKinley such a wonderful community in which to grow from fledgling attorney to the 25th President of the United States.

Finally to my wife, Bonnie, for putting up with my curmudgeonly ways while I fought off the deadline for this book. Kid, you're the **best!**

INTRODUCTION

Pioneers and adventurers heading west from Columbiana, Ohio, fought their way through heavy forest until they reached the hilltop where Trump Road intersects Lincoln Street today. At that point, they broke through the foliage to find a broad clearing ranging west, nearly to present-day Massillon. It was in this cleared area that a surveyor, Bezaleel Wells, (picture on p. 2) made a most fortuitous purchase. He bought the land sight unseen, and found that it was a town planner's dream, as it had ample supplies of water and lumber on its perimeter.

The origin of the name Canton has never been explained. Was it named for Canton, China, or the name given to the Baltimore, Maryland estate of a friend of Wells, or from the name given to counties in Switzerland? To this day, no one knows.

Bezaleel Wells laid out his town according to the plat map pictured on p. 8. He ceded three plots for specific use to the city—one for a courthouse, one for a school, and one for a cemetery. To this day, the Stark County Courthouse is on its plot, Timken Senior High School is on the original school plot, and the cemetery plot is now a small city park, but when the cemetery was moved, one grave marker was left in place to assure compliance with Mr. Wells's wishes.

During the early to mid-nineteenth century, Canton and Stark County became hotbeds for the manufacture of farm implements. And why not—Ohio was the leading agricultural center of the country. Canals were built to get our grains to market, and, later, railroads passed through here for the same reason. We were the hub of the American universe, agriculturally at least.

With rampant industrial expansion, there was a need for more people. An immigrant explosion occurred, and Canton soon had Italians, Greeks, Spanish, Romanians, Russians, Poles, and Jews from many European countries. Each group brought its own cultural practices and specialty consumer goods. We have all become an incredibly diverse population because of their immigration to our community.

Farm implement production went west with the population expansion in that direction, but Canton has always been a resilient community. The steel industry became a major employer in the area, as we have the one commodity that other regions lack—water. Our rivers, streams, and lakes provide an abundance of that resource, which assures industrial growth. The fact that we have always had a preponderance of dreamers who have created work when old industry has let us down has also helped our hometown. Frank Case invented a dental chair, which spawned the Weber Dental Company in 1876. Henry S. Belden went to the American Centennial celebration in Philadelphia and came home with a new process for mass producing durable bricks, and the Belden Brick Company became an enduring enterprise. When local creativity was not creating jobs fast enough, the business community formed the board of trade, which was much like the modern-day chamber of commerce, to induce companies to relocate in Canton. From their efforts, John Dueber combined his two companies, the Dueber Watch Works and the Hampden Watch Case Company, into the Dueber-Hampden Watch Company, and provided jobs from the 1880s to 1930. Not satisfied with that effort, the board went to St. Louis and convinced an inventor to bring his fledgling tapered roller bearing company to Canton to be closer to the heart of the burgeoning automobile industry. The Timken Company is the bright shining result. No community could have a better corporate citizen!

Republic Steel and the United States Steel Companies have located plants in Canton. Though both are now gone, they were an integral part of our community. Even a pharmacist found this city to be profitable beyond his wildest dreams. H.H. Ink started a drugstore on East Tuscarawas Street and parlayed that into the Tonsilene Company. From his profits came the Palace Theater in 1926, a gift to the city which he loved.

Canton has seen its ups and downs. Since the late 1960s, it has seen a steady erosion of businesses from downtown to the suburban shopping malls—most noticeably Belden Village Mall, which has now taken on the appearance of a small city. There have been many attempts to resurrect the downtown, and most have come up short in results. Today there are more and more voices calling for a return of businesses and professionals to the city. Nowhere is that mantra heard louder than from the office of Mayor Richard D. Watkins. The second voice in that chorus is that of the Canton Preservation Society, which has put its money where its mouth is by purchasing for redevelopment the east side of the 200 block of Market Avenue North, and the venerable Landmark building, and the rest of the block on which it sits. Much is to be done, but plans are afoot, and by the time of the publication of this book, construction may well have begun on the 200 block of Market Avenue.

This rather faded picture (*left*) is of the original plat for the city which Mr. Wells laid out. He gave the city three plots of land for specific usage—one was for a courthouse, one for a school, and one for a cemetery. Today, all three are still being utilized as directed, although the cemetery is now a small park, but one headstone remains in place to fulfill Mr. Wells's legacy. There have been three courthouses on the plot so designated, and here (*right*) are two of the three schools on the West Tuscarawas Street school property, which now houses Timken Senior High School.

8

One

CITYSCAPE

This photo, from March 1867, shows that preservation is not a new phenomenon. Taken from the city square looking down East Tuscarawas Street, there seems to be a house in the middle of the street. However, on closer inspection, we can see a foundation just behind the house. As it turns out, the house was being relocated to facilitate the construction of the George D. Harter Bank.

Mr. Alfred Hurford and a bartender are pictured in front of the Hurford House Hotel, which was known as the St. Cloud Hotel from its construction in 1868, but was renamed in honor of Mr. Hurford at the request of President William McKinley, Canton's number one citizen until his assassination in 1901. The Hurford House was razed in that same year, to make way for the Courtland Hotel.

The completed Courtland is shown about 1920. It stood on the corner of West Tuscarawas Street and Court Avenue until 1992. With much controversy, the St. Francis Hotel (its name had been changed), which served for many years as the Stark County Office Building, was razed to make way for an underground parking garage.

Cornelius Aultman built this magnificent home, which passed in ownership to Kate Aultman, his widow. She willed the estate to her step-daughter, Elizabeth Aultman Harter, the wife of George D. Harter, and thereafter it became known as the Harter Estate. It stood on 11 acres on Market Avenue North at 11th Street. Unfortunately, the house became the victim of urban renewal and was replaced by this complex—the Cultural Center for the Arts (below).

The center houses the Players Guild, Canton Ballet, Canton Symphony, and the Canton Museum of Art—all wonderful additions to the Canton community. It does seem a shame that such a magnificent structure could not have been saved.

The Shooting Club, pictured here, is one of several that proliferated during the Victorian Era. Here they are posing, in 1895, at Nimisilla Park, which later became the home of the Canton Zoo. Seated third from the right is Louis Miday, the uncle of Ruth Whitticar, a longtime Cantonian whose father, Eugene, is responsible for several of the more unique photographs in this book. These avid hunters undoubtedly enjoyed their group outings when hunting near this rural mill.

The Henry Mill was located at the corner of 38th Street and Guilford Avenue Northwest, near the railroad tracks, for much of the nineteenth century. It no longer stands, but was once a busy center for milling grain grown in the area. The four-man workforce is barely discernible at the entrance of the mill.

In the 1880s, bicycling was all the rage among the genteel set in Canton. The Canton Bicycle Club was founded on July 25, 1883, and incorporated on April 25, 1887. The officers (inset) were C.W. Keplinger (president), Guy Tilden (vice president), Will G. Saxton (secretary and treasurer), C.L. Oberly (captain), H.A. Trump (1st lieutenant), and E. Barrie (2nd lieutenant).

These "daring" young men pedaled their ungainly highwheeler and lowboy bicycles all over the city, and one or two of them may be seen riding up Third and Market Avenue South in 1884. The twin peaks of the courthouse and the Kenney Brothers Store, which advertised as having "everything you need," are also visible. That slogan can be seen above the striped canopy over the windows.

While many of the most famous actors and actresses of the Victorian era played at Canton's Grand Opera House, local programs were also performed there. This is the cast for *In Honor Bound,* performed in 1891 or 1892. The cast included from left to right: William Kuhas, Evelyn Phillips, Lieutenant Colonel Harry Frease, and Cora Martin. These local productions always commanded a large audience, as everyone wanted to see their friends and relatives on the stage of Canton's showplace for theatrical arts. This theater was the scene of the last concert given by the great Enrico Caruso on his last tour of America. He made this performance for the Sons of Italy Lodge in Canton.

In 1884, Canton joined the nineteenth century with its first mass transportation system—the horse-drawn trolley. Pictured here at the central barn of the Canton Street Car Lines on West Tuscarawas Street are the conductors, groomsmen, and blacksmiths. It was not until 1889 that the first electric trolley system began operating around the city and some surrounding areas. The paving of Canton's streets in brick by Henry S. Belden began about this same time, but started on East Tuscarawas Street, and had not yet reached the west side of town. We do know that this picture was taken in the spring of the year, as the conductor on the car is carrying his straw hat, a sure harbinger of spring and summer.

These early trolleys made many runs daily to the Dueber Hampden Watchworks on Dueber Avenue Southwest. In one of the early corporate raids, Canton's Board of Trade (forerunner of the chamber of commerce) heard that John Dueber was in the market to consolidate his two businesses, the Dueber Watch Company in Covington, Kentucky, and the Hampden Watch Case Company in Springfield, Massachusetts. The board raised $100,000 in three months, and secured 25 acres of land for the plant site. Ground was broken in 1886 for the twin buildings. At its peak, Dueber-Hampden employed 2,300 people. By 1930, they were unable to compete with the several watchmakers which had consolidated, and the business was sold to the Soviet Union. The buildings stood, used as storage facilities, until the late 1950s, when they were razed for a discount department store.

Though not from Canton, Jacob Sechler Coxey led an "army" of unemployed men to Washington, D.C. in 1894, during a desperate financial "panic" (the Panic of '93) nearly as bad as the Great Depression of the 1930s. Their demand was truly radical, as they were asking the government for unemployment insurance to tide them over until times got better. President Cleveland was not impressed, and had government troops drive the men out of town and arrested Coxey after a comical chase across the Capitol steps and lawn. This photo shows the march passing by the workhouse in Canton's northeast end. Mr. Coxey was not a poor man by any means, in fact he was quite wealthy and somewhat eccentric, having named his son Legal Tender, but having come from modest beginnings, he identified with the downtrodden and pledged his best efforts in assisting them in their "just cause." Mr. Coxey is believed to be the gentleman riding on the white horse behind the African-American man carrying the flag.

The Stark County Courthouse is pictured here prior to its second refurbishment. This photo was probably taken before 1884, as there are no trolley tracks in view, and Henry Belden's paving bricks have not made their way from East Tuscarawas Street. Notice the fountain next to the city bank sign at the base of the courthouse annex, another structure which has been lost due to a lack of proper maintenance.

It was a short walk to the courthouse for the young attorneys who made their homes in the Barnett House Hotel on the southeast corner of East Tuscarawas Street and Cherry Avenue. In the tradition of the times, the Barnett House was very comfortable, so as to appeal to the many long-term residents who came to town by train and sought to establish themselves in our community. As was the case with many hotels, Barnett House was named for its proprietor, Eudoist Barnett. It was the center of social activity in the 1890s. Henry S. Belden's Belden Brick Company laid the very first paving brick in Canton in front of the Barnett House in the 1880s. Mr. Belden had attended the United State's Centennial celebration in Philadelphia in 1876 and observed a new and efficient method for mass producing bricks. He brought the process back to Canton, and with our area's abundant clay he established one of Canton's most enduring companies.

Prepared for his place in a local celebration is this representative for Moxie, a purported "nerve food" beverage. If its contents were like the original Coca Cola, it might well have contained cocaine or other stimulants as a base ingredient. Thompson and Young were the local distributors for this liquid refresher.

Canton residents could have purchased their Moxie at this store, Wyant and Noel, which stood on the corner of Cleveland Avenue and Twelfth Street Northwest in 1895. The store had a cropped corner, and in keeping with that tradition, Anderson's Flower Shop, which is on the same site, also features the same cropping. Wyant and Noel was a very important store in the winter, as it had a telephone, and in the winter local ice-skating enthusiasts would call to see if Feather Pond (located between Market and Cleveland Avenues) was frozen. There was a streetcar route from the Square that terminated in front of the store. Mr. C.W. Noel is on the extreme right of the picture below.

This is the original Canton City Hall, and in the rear is the central fire station, which stood on Cleveland Avenue Southwest until the 1950s. The city outgrew the capacity of the building, as the demands of a modern progressive city outstripped the space available. It has been replaced by this cold and austere chrome and glass complex, which has separate facilities for the municipal court, city council, and the police department.

Pictured here is the Grand Army of the Republic Band marching on South Market Avenue. It was one of many community bands that were prevalent during the post-Civil War and Victorian eras and appealed to community pride. The band was formed in 1866 by Civil War veterans and played on for 61 years, disbanding in 1927. Fred Yost, who had been the youngest drummer boy in the Union Army, was still an active participant with the band. The GAR group was known as McKinley's Good Luck Band, as they appeared with him frequently, and especially on election nights. The band marched one last time for "the Major" at the dedication of his memorial in 1907.

The attraction of being a member of the Grand Army of the Republic led Canton Mayor Ed Bour to become a drum major, performing during his time in office.

Two

MCKINLEY

William McKinley, the 25th President of the United States, was Canton's biggest claim to fame. Mr. McKinley was decorated for bravery three times during the Civil War for his efforts in troop support, most notably at the Battle of Antietam Creek. After the war, he completed studies in law and at the behest of his sister Anna, he located in the booming city of Canton. He frequented one of the city's banks and was smitten by a female teller, Ida Saxton, who's father owned the bank. As the story goes he pursued Ida until she caught him. They were married on January 25, 1871, and began a long and devoted life together—one that alternately held triumph and tragedy. They had two daughters who died very young—baby Ida at six months and Katie at three years. Mrs. McKinley then went into a life-long depression, but fulfilled her duties to her beloved William as he rose politically from county prosecutor, to the United States Congress, to governor, and finally to the White House.

Here is a corner view of the McKinley's home at 143 North Market Avenue, which was a wedding present from Ida's father.

The McKinleys, however, did not live in that house very long. They moved in on their wedding day in 1871, but after the deaths of their daughters, Mrs. McKinley could not bear the sad memories surrounding her every day. They sold the home and moved in with her sister Mary (known in the family as Pina) in the house that her father, James Saxton, owned on South Market Avenue. As the McKinleys were out of town frequently (he served eight terms in congress and two as governor), they were little bother to Pina and her husband, Marshall C. Barber. After Mr. McKinley's second term as Governor of Ohio, he and Ida re-purchased the North Market property for their retirement home.

In 1896, William McKinley answered his party's (Republican) call and accepted the nomination for president. Due to Ida's precarious physical health, Bill waged his campaign from the front porch of their Market Avenue North home. The party-faithful were brought to Canton by train, financed largely by Marcus Hanna, who was a very wealthy industrialist from Cleveland. This picture is of Illinois Day, September 18, 1896. Mr. McKinley was apprised of who was coming so he could tailor his speeches to their interests. As each group arrived at the train station on South Market, they marched up the street with great fanfare making every day, except Sunday, seem like the Fourth of July.

In a mysterious photograph taken on October 26, 1896, during the campaign, this group of celebrants is marching under an arch built especially for the campaign on North Market Avenue, near the candidate's home. If you look closely at the treetop in the upper right-hand corner of the picture, you will see two men tied in the tree. It is suspected that they were there as some form of punishment, but no one has yet been able to find any record of such a sentence in the existing court records or in any newspaper accounts.

There were times during his presidential campaign that Mr. McKinley had to stand on a box to be seen by the large crowds which came to hear his message of "Sound Money" based on the gold standard. His opponent, William Jennings Bryan, was the leading exponent for the free coinage of silver, hence his nickname, "the Silver-Tongued Orator."

Shown here, after one of his many speeches, the President speaks to the individual concerns of a constituent. The house became Mercy Hospital until the late 1920s, when its expansion forced the city to move it to a park near what is now Heritage Christian School. There it sat, deteriorating, until a 1934 condemnation order from the board of health was issued. On January 30, 1935, it was razed, and a heritage came to an abrupt end.

After Mr. McKinley won his election in 1896, there were at least as many visitors as there had been during the campaign, many of whom were office seekers, as the Republicans had been out of power in Washington for four years. To help insulate the President-elect from unnecessary intrusions as he began selecting a cabinet, these men (above) helped keep unwanted office seekers away from Mr. McKinley. Standing next to Mr. McKinley is his easiest choice, William R. Day, who became his secretary of state. After the assassination, President Theodore Roosevelt named Mr. Day to the Supreme Court.

The President never forgot who his friends were. He dined with Marcus Hanna at his Cleveland home whenever his duties as Chief Executive led him to that city. He also facilitated the appointment of Mr. Hanna as a United States Senator. It was not until 1912 that direct election of senators became law.

Although the President had seen enough carnage during his Civil War service, he was unable to stop the nation from being drawn into what became known as the Spanish-American War. Mr. McKinley became a major during his service in the Civil War, due to his valorous efforts at the Battle of Antietam Creek. The Major, as he liked to be called, had several detractors who chose to call him "Coffee Bill," owing to his duties as a mess sergeant before his promotion. This memorial obelisk, honoring him, stands on the battlefield. His reluctance caused his future vice president, Theodore Roosevelt, to claim that McKinley had no more backbone than a chocolate eclair, a comment he recanted in time to become the vice-presidential candidate in 1900. Mr. McKinley's first vice president, Garret Hobart of New Jersey, died in 1899.

The war lasted three or four months and allowed Mr. Roosevelt to become a hero for his "charge" up San Juan Hill in Cuba. This is the Eighth Ohio Volunteer Infantry, known as McKinley's Own, receiving a hero's welcome from their fellow Cantonians upon their return from service in Cuba.

Mr. McKinley sits on his porch with an assistant, who waits for McKinley's next request. Judging by his formal attire and top hat perched on his head, one would assume that it was a Sunday. Mr. McKinley, being so deeply religious, would do precious little to break the Sabbath. During his campaign in 1896, a group of supporters showed up at his home on a Sunday expecting to hear the great man speak to their concerns. What they received was an invitation to attend church services with him and nothing else.

The President is pictured here entering his church on July 8, 1901. It was one of his last trips home before the ill-fated trip to Buffalo. A devoutly religious man, he served as president of his Sunday school class until he left for Washington in March of 1897 to be inaugurated President of the United States (it was not until 1937 that the inauguration of the President was moved from March 5 to January 20).

Shortly after his second term in the White House, the President and Mrs. McKinley set out on a western tour of America, visiting mines in the Arizona and New Mexico territories and California. Upon his return, he made good on a promise to visit the Pan American Exposition in Buffalo, New York, much to the chagrin of Mrs. McKinley. On September 6, he made a speech on the grounds of the fair and spent some time greeting the people visiting. An anarchist named Leon Czolgosz (pronounced Cholgosh) shot the President to the astonishment of all. His wounds were not considered fatal, but the medical staff in attendance were unable to find the bullet lodged deeply in his abdominal area, and eight days later he died, not from the wound but from advancing gangrene. Mr. Czolgosz was tried, found guilty, and executed within six weeks of the assassination.

This train brought the slain President's body home for the last time. It had lain in state in the Capitol rotunda for the people of Washington to pay their last respects. Its arrival signaled an end of an era in Canton, as it would no longer have the political impact of being the residence of the nation's chief executive.

The period of public mourning in Canton began at the train station and carried on throughout the city. Here photographers and press people sought out the best vantage spots for their reportage of the somber occasion. The hearse is barely visible. Theodore Roosevelt, the new president, is in this print, following behind the hearse in a carriage. On the far right, obscuring Mr. Roosevelt, are moving picture cameras.

Mr. McKinley's casket was placed in his North Market Avenue home prior to the funeral services. Here it has been placed on the hearse with full military and Masonic honors being paid. The President had been an active Freemason, participating in the York Rite and Scottish Rite. The men in the fringed headgear are his fellow York Rite brethren. The arch in the background was one of four that were hastily constructed at the four corners of entry to the city immediately after the assassination.

The President's body is borne into the First Methodist Church (now Church of the Savior) through the east door, with all mourners showing the utmost respect. One can barely discern the Knights Templar honor guard at the end of the procession.

This is the view looking west on Tuscarawas Street on September 20, 1901, during President McKinley's funeral cortege. The Courtland Hotel can be partially seen in the left of the picture. This hotel later became the St. Frances Hotel, and finally became the Stark County Office Building.

President McKinley's body was placed in the Werts Receiving Vault in West Lawn Cemetery, as the family had not made any preparations for his death. The body lay in the vault until 1907, when a suitable memorial was erected. It remained there for those six years, with full military guard around the clock.

A committee was formed to decide where the monument would be located and what design would be most in keeping with the memory of the man. Here the committee, headed by Mr. McKinley's secretary, George Cortelyou, is selecting the site where the slain President will be memorialized. It is high on a hill, overlooking the city which he loved like none other.

From the top of the hill, there is a panorama of the city below. It is little wonder that this spot was the favorite of the McKinleys for picnics throughout the course of their lives in Canton. The prominence of this site was the deciding factor in the committee's decision to use it as the site for the memorial.

Many Italian stonemasons were employed to build this monument. In fact, several were brought to Canton from their homeland to work on the structure. Celebrated for their skills in stone work, many stayed on in Canton to establish their own businesses as stonemasons and cement contractors.

In 1906, the monument was beginning to take shape, along with the 96 steps to the top. That number was specified, as that was the year in which Mr. McKinley was elected president. The last photo was taken during the final phase of construction in the summer of 1907. All that was missing was the statue of the slain President, which was cast in bronze and was in place in time for the dedication ceremony. It depicts Mr. McKinley as he made his last speech.

September 30, 1907, was the date that the McKinley Monument was dedicated. President Theodore Roosevelt returned to Canton to make a memorial speech. Theodore Roosevelt is dwarfed by the dome of the memorial. He would have recalled the slain President as a man of peace. Inscribed inside the dome is the "tag line" from his last speech: "Let us ever remember that our interest is in concord not conflict and that our real eminence rests in the victories of peace not those of war." It is in these words that the President who led the country into its first international war of the modern age, albeit reluctantly, and defeated an entrenched European power, would wish to be remembered.

On May 26, 1907, Mrs. McKinley passed away. She would never see the beautiful, but simple, monument to her William. They lie side by side in dual Vermont Green Granite Sarcophagi, pictured here with a funeral wreath in front. In the rear of the rotunda, interred in the walls, are the McKinley's two daughters, Ida and Katie.

Three

TWENTIETH CENTURY CITYSCAPE

West Tuscarawas Street was the setting, around the turn of the century, for these three electric automobiles, two of which seem to be either advertising or carrying pianos for Burgener's piano store. This store's history has been lost, but the A.E. Stocker Tobacco Store lasted well into the twentieth century.

In 1901, the Steiner Wholesale Coal Company and the J.L. Maurer Drug Store and office building were leveled to make way for an F.W. Woolworth 5 and 10 cent store. This was a prime retail space for a variety store such as a five and dime, as they were called. Barely visible on the left is the Kenney Brothers Dry Goods Store, and Dumont's Groceries and Provisions is on the right. This block would be nearly unrecognizable to anyone from that era, as all those structures have been replaced by the Newmarket Parking Garage. In fact, the City National Bank building (not pictured) is the only original (?) structure left on the block. The Canton Floral store is on the corner of 2nd and Market South, but is in a structure cut down from its original four stories.

A.H. "Tony" Wilson owned the first Cadillac dealership in Canton. "Tony's" building originally housed a Winton dealership. If you look closely, the Winton logo can be seen to the right of the Cadillac sign even though an attempt was made to whitewash it. His building, at 514 Cleveland Avenue Northwest, still stands.

This is "Tony" proving, or showing off, the power of theses machines by pulling 8.5 tons on Market Avenue North. The four-story building in the rear was the St. Edward Hotel, built in 1896. That structure still stands today, on the corner of 4th Street and Market Avenue, and is known as the Centennial building. Unfortunately, the cluster of buildings next to "Tony's" Caddy is now a parking lot.

The Case and Davis Mansions have a unique legend behind them. Zebulon Davis began his career as an entrepreneur in Cleveland, inventing several gasoline-powered products: a lamp, a stove, an engine for automobiles, and, most notably, the first carburetor for the early Winton automobiles. He also helped found the Standard Lighting Company in Cleveland and served as its president for some 39 years. Zeb formed the Diamond Portland Cement Company in Middlebranch, a rural community northeast of Canton, in 1892. Mr Frank Case was a disgruntled lawyer who moved on to produce one of the finest dental chairs in the country. His company, which was later known as Weber Dental Company, was highly successful.

Legend has it that Mr. Davis and Mr. Case were in love with the same lady, and she issued the challenge that whichever one of them built the largest house would win her hand in marriage. Mr. Case won, and Zeb Davis remained a bachelor until his death in 1931 at 87 years of age. It should be added that he never completed the construction of his home.

Zebulon Davis is pictured here with two unidentified women (one of them could be the lady who spurned his proposal because Mr. Case built the larger home), motoring in the first automobile in Canton—a Winton of course!

Perhaps old Zeb was taking the ladies to the new Canton Auditorium. The completion of this wonder of its age led to the ultimate destruction of the Grand Opera House. The auditorium was located on Cleveland and Court Avenues between 4th and 5th Streets Northwest. Today, the site is, unfortunately, a parking lot.

In 1903, Old Bill Simpson's Smokery and Chewery used a novel advertising approach to attract customers. Located on the corner of West 8th Street (3rd Southwest today) and South Market, Pauline the cow grazed as astonished customers looked on, after buying their tobacco products of course. Mr. Simpson is the gentleman on the left, in the doorway, standing next to Charles Kirkland.

May 7, 1904, brought a cultural event which sent excitement coursing through the veins of every child in Canton. The Walter L. Main Circus came to town! This is the grand parade which all circuses staged in every city in which they appeared. They are marching up South Market to the square, then east on Tuscarawas Street, then north on Cherry Avenue to Second Street, then west to Market again, and, finally, west on Tuscarawas to the fairgrounds, where they performed several shows. Given the wanderlust of small boys of those times, one wonders how many may have run away to join the circus.

The Dannemiller Grocery Company was a Canton Institution for more than 75 years, from its founding in 1869. Their Royal Blend Coffee was brewed all over town, in homes, and in restaurants, and its piquant aroma could be savored on city streets any time of the day or night. This delivery truck is in front of the last Dannemiller warehouse. There had been several warehouses, and given the construction of that truck, one must wonder how any product packaged in glass containers arrived unbroken—it has solid rubber tires and no signs of any springs or other sus pension system.

This rather austere-looking gentleman is Guy Tilden, who was Canton's premiere architect from his arrival in town in 1883, until his retirement in 1924. There have been so many homes, churches, and commercial buildings with his imprimatur on them that it is hard to remember them all without a detailed list. We do know that very few remain, and some of those are in jeopardy. Among the commissions he executed are the Trinity Lutheran Church on West Tuscarawas Street, the Weber Dental Building on Mahoning Road Northeast, and the Carnegie Library, which today houses the Timken Foundation. Some of his buildings which have been razed are the McKinley Hotel, the Dime Bank, the Case Mansion, and Kobacher's Department Store on Market Avenue North. Market Avenue is now home of the last Guy Tilden House, as the Canton Preservation Society helped facilitate the move of the house, saving it from certain demolition on Cleveland Avenue Northwest, where the construction of a new drugstore threatened it. The house now proudly sits on a site at 17th Street and Market Avenue North.

Today, 318 Cherry Avenue Northeast is the home of Daniel Quinlan's Lowry Lithograph Company, but in the early 1920s it was the home of S.W. Cashner Motorcar Company. Mr. Cashner sold White Pleasure Cars and Trucks and Stearns-Knight Pleasure Cars.

This is the entire Canton Fire Department as it existed in October of 1913. They are arrayed from the courthouse, south on Market Avenue, towards the McKinley Hotel. At the extreme right of the picture is that old pumper, the Daniel Worley. It was a time of transition for the

Local automobile dealer George W. Monnot was one of those individuals who frightened the trolley workers, as he introduced a vehicle which would put every other transportation worker out of a job. It was none other than the Hydro-Car! This monstrosity was built in 1917, and it was three vehicles in one: a car, a truck, and a boat. It is shown on a Canton

department, as it was made up of some horse-drawn and some motorized vehicles. These were extremely brave individuals, as they faced all the dangers of fire at that time with equipment that would never pass inspection in the most backward countries today.

street and on the waters of Meyers Lake. If you look closely, Mr. Monnot's son Georgie can be seen behind the driver in the car configuration and on the prow of the boat. The prow became the rear of the vehicle when on land. Luckily, it was simply too advanced for its time and was quickly forgotten.

There was one way to avoid those chuckholes in the streets. All you had to do was jump on board one of the Canton Streetcar Lines' trolleys that these gentlemen drove all over town, and even across the county. These hard-working men gave a superior effort every day to make sure that Canton's citizenry received an enjoyable ride—otherwise the newly-arrived automobile would put them out of a job.

The Timken Company began in St. Louis, where Mr. Timken had an idea for a tapered roller bearing, which would greatly reduce friction on the wheels of trains. He soon discovered that those bearings would enhance the reliability of the "new-fangled" automobile, and he wanted to locate closer to the heart of the burgeoning auto industry. The Canton Board of Trade facilitated the location of the Timken Roller Bearing Company to Canton around 1899. Canton has been enriched immeasurably by the presence of the Timken Company and family. The city has benefited not only by the thousands of jobs the company provides, but also culturally through the gift of our beautiful Cultural Center for the Arts, which houses our Civic Opera Company, Player's Guild, Canton Museum of Art, and the Canton Ballet. The train is the famous Timken Four Aces, which served as proof of the reliability of Timken's tapered roller bearings for many years.

Transportation in Canton took on many forms, mostly motorized, but William Martin was one of Canton's first airplane pilots. He is shown here flying his bi-plane, c. 1915. Notice the propellers, seemingly frozen in time, and also note the chain and gears reaching out to the propellers—yet there is no sign of an engine. Mr. Martin claimed he never put a motor in his planes, but he did leave space for one if a buyer wished to add that accouterment. This plane is currently stored at the McKinley Museum of History, Science, and Industry on a "temporary" loan from the Smithsonian Institution.

Canton industrialist H.H. Timken is shown with the first company airplane, a Ford Tri-Motor. The plane was demonstrating take-off and landing at either of the two airfields in Canton: McKinley Airport, which was at the site of the present-day Mahoning Road Shopping Center, or Sherrick Field, which was located where McKinley Senior High School sits today.

The Timken Gate House is about all that remains of the palatial estate that Mr. Timken built and later donated for the site of the former Timken Mercy Hospital. The gatehouse sits along a small stream in the Canton City Parks and will someday be refurbished to its former splendor.

Harry Renkert owned the Metropolitan Brick Company, which was famous for its paving bricks. Mr. Renkert, however, believed that those bricks were more versatile than their use for street paving. To answer his critics, he had the Renkert Building constructed. It was Canton's first skyscraper, standing ten stories high, and covered entirely in paving brick! This monument to Harry Renkert's belief proudly stands today in downtown Canton as a viable business office tower.

During the height of Prohibition, Canton earned its nickname of "Little Chicago," as there was rampant corruption in the community. A mayor and his brother were removed from office, and this stern-looking gent, Donald Ring Mellett, an editor of the *Canton Daily News*, spent his short time in Canton calling out the corrupt to account for their misdeeds. On July 26, 1926, he was rewarded for his vigilance with a bullet in the back of his head. The chief of police was convicted of being involved in the murder, but acquitted later after a retrial in a different community. The former chief of detectives and three local thugs spent the rest of their lives in prison for the murder.

Steineck Bakery trucks poised for delivery during the 1930s.

Hirscheimer's Clothier was located on the square for nearly 50 years, until about 1924, when Walker's bought them out and assumed the location. A gentleman was simply not perceived as such unless he wore a Hart, Schaffner, and Marx suit from Hirscheimer's. This picture was taken around 1923.

The northeast corner of 6th and Market Avenue North was the location of the Hotel Northern. Very few of us remember the hotel by any name other than the Belden Hotel, which also housed the Knights of Pythias Lodge. Even more important to many Cantonians was the Purple Cow Restaurant on the first floor of the Belden. It was a popular hangout for those who appreciated good food that was priced economically. Unfortunately, the diminishing need for downtown hotels led to its demise, and today the vacant lot is for sale.

This is a view of Canton we would very much like to see once again. The hustle and bustle of Cantonians walking on the 200 block of Market Avenue North as pictured in this photo from the mid-1940s. Every storefront from Shirley Shoes south has been razed, and a parking lot is all that remains in that space.

Much has changed in the history of Aultman Hospital since this photo was taken. Starting as a small, two-story building at 2600 6th Street Southwest, it has grown to encompass an entire city block, with another block used just for its parking garage.

Canton was once home to this magnificent Pennsylvania station, but the lack of ridership caused it to fall into disuse, and ultimately the wrecking ball made an unwelcome appearance. Like many other wonderful buildings in Canton, it is lost for all time.

Of all the beautiful buildings on Market Avenue, the one shining example of preservation in our city is the Palace Theater. The theater is visible in this mid-1950s view of Market Avenue, looking south from 7th Street. The Palace Theater was a gift to the city by H.H. Ink, a highly successful pharmacist around the turn of the century. Mr. Ink developed a sore throat remedy he called Tonsilene, which featured a giraffe suffering from a sore throat as its logo. The Renkert building and Loews Theater are the only other identifiable structures in this view.

For many years, the Canton JayCees operated this civic project, which was Mother Goose Land located on West Tuscarawas Street. The park was a very nice place for parents to take their children to see such attractions as the little red schoolhouse and the whale. Suburban sprawl led to its ultimate demise. Many of the characters can be seen today at the Sluggers and Putter entertainment complex in Canal Fulton.

Canton and Stark County have become known as bellwether political communities—almost always voting for the presidential winner. In these photos, Richard Nixon campaigns for the presidency in 1960 on the square of North Canton. The store in the background has since been replaced by a bank.

Mr. Nixon is addressing a rally in the Canton Auditorium. Mr. Nixon did not pay enough attention to the Canton area, and lost his bid to succeed President Eisenhower by a razor-thin margin to John F. Kennedy. It was a mistake he did not repeat in 1968 or 1972, as he won handily in those years.

Call it ego, or what you will, but I could not resist including this picture of the author. This is Ronald E. Sterling with his sister Teri back in April 1955. Check out those cool Billy the kid SafeT Knee blue jeans.

Four

THE GREEK COMMUNITY

In 1898, the first Greek immigrant arrived in Canton. George Loukas was a tailor by trade and a trailblazer by accident. It was not long before hundreds of his fellow Greeks came to Canton seeking the American Dream. By 1913, there was a need to establish an Orthodox church. A priest was already in Canton, and he assisted the faithful in their building campaign. Although he was called away before the building began, the Reverend Leonidas Athamakos served as the first priest of the St. Haralambos Parish from 1913 to 1919. Rather than have harsh feelings over the name of the church, all suggested names were placed in a hat and St. Haralambos was drawn. Reverend Athamakos's daughter Pauline married one of the originators of the church, Gust Niarchos, and when her father left, she remained in Canton to see the fruit of his efforts become reality.

These new immigrants proved to be very industrious, and that manifested into various businesses. This young man, Frank Mergus, started working for Mr. Elite in the restaurant business and eventually became the owner of the famed Mergus Restaurant in the Onesto Hotel. During a more unenlightened time, Mr. Mergus had to return to his training as a waiter when the great singer Marian Anderson was staying in the hotel and none of his waiters would serve an African American. Frank Mergus was always a class act in Canton.

Many immigrants started small groceries or other necessary businesses in their own neighborhoods to serve those who had not mastered the English language. This store, located at 733 Cherry Avenue Southeast, was owned by George and Angeline Goglos. Mr. Goglos was very dedicated to his Greek heritage and sponsored many fellow Cretans' emigration to America. George and his niece, Margaret Koufos, operated the poultry market next to the grocery.

Anastasios Koufos, his wife, Margaret, and his daughter Mary, are pictured here around 1930. In addition to Margaret operating the poultry market, Anastasios also worked at the Timken Roller Bearing Company.

The Greek school was a very important part of the immigrant experience. It was operated as a means to help maintain the language and culture of the Greek homeland among the children who were assimilating into the new American culture. This group photo was taken around 1936 or 1937. Included in the picture are Nick Barry, who has gained notoriety for his portrayal of Ebenezer Scrooge in Dickens's *A Christmas Carol* for many years, and James Marinos, the fine dry cleaner who founded Glotone Cleaners. Marinos was killed in a tragic auto accident. The Bozeka brothers, Angelo and Steve, are also seen in this photo. Steve was, for many years, the spotter for Frank Gifford on Monday Night Football. Demetrios Economides was the teacher of this class.

St. Haralambos's weddings always brought out large crowds, and the wedding of Pete and Helen Mentzelos in 1928 was no exception. Anastasios Koufos is in the fourth row from the bottom and third from the right—he is heavy-set, mustachioed, and slightly balding.

Pictured here is a group of World War II veterans of Greek descent, marching in the 1947 Memorial Day parade down Market Avenue. These proud sons of Canton's first Greek immigrants fought bravely to protect their new homeland, and marched in many of these parades.

Here in a local cemetery, these same veterans are paying homage to their fallen comrades. The bugler is George Papadapoulos, who later became Stark County Sheriff. He had been advised that he would have a better chance of winning election to that office if he changed that long, ethnic last name to Murphy, but George was intensely proud of his heritage and would not hear of it. He won several elections and carried the nickname of "Murph" around the sheriff's department.

St. Haralambos Parish grew by fits and starts, and by the 1950s, the building was too small and no longer convenient for the vast majority of parishioners. Many of the parishioners were returning World War II veterans who had moved out of the city. A new church building was deemed too costly, and a decision had to be made. The church members decided to move it from the original site at 6th and Walnut Avenue Southeast to a newly acquired parcel of land at the corner of 25th Street and Harvard Avenue Northwest.

The original plan was to move the building intact, even though it was becoming too small. However, the church was too heavy for the streets and infrastructure, and another decision had to be made. The next idea was to cut it in half and sacrifice a 16-foot section from the middle. Concurrent with that plan was to add a 48-foot section in the middle. That would replace the missing 16 feet and add room for the growth of the parish.

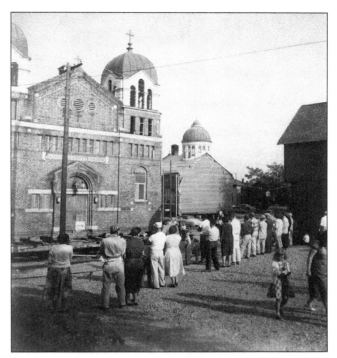

Mural and Son, of Cleveland, was selected as the mover. On Saturday, June 14, 1958, at 2:29 p.m., the big move began. The church was slowly separated and began its move to 25th Street and Harvard Avenue Northwest. The "sidewalk superintendents" were treated to a strange view as the sections parted company. The newly separated church buildings were on the same site, but one was moving! The back half of the structure went first, as it was the heaviest.

St. Haralambos Church was an ungainly sight as it moved through Canton's streets. There were two points where the church nearly tumbled—one was at the intersection of Market and Tuscarawas, when it inexplicably started to lean. The mover later said that one more degree of tilt would have caused the building to fall off the dollies to become a pile of rubble.

The second near tragedy was at 30th Street and Cleveland Avenue Northwest, where the intersection was highly uneven. Winch lines snapped, and the building slid backwards some three feet before workmen could halt it. It took 18 days for the back half to arrive at 25th and Harvard.

With the back half placed on footers at the new site, the second, or front half, began to move north. Covering the same route, there were no additional problems. Mural and Son had learned from the misadventures and near tragedies involved with the first section's move. This section was much lighter and took only eight days to move.

After both sections were placed on the new foundation, the construction of the new midsection began. Work continued long into the winter, as Mural and Son had promised that the new structure would be completed by February of 1959. It was to be 48 feet long, to replace the original 16 feet lost to the move and to add 32 feet to allow for the future growth of the parish.

These faithful believers attended the first services held in the new location. It was just like a brand new church, with its addition in the middle and the freshly sandblasted exterior, now free of the grime which had built up from decades of being in the heart of Canton's industrial sector.

On March 1, 1959, the completed church was turned over to the parish and a proud congregation met for its first service in the old/new building. The sense of pride and achievement is evident in these two views of that first service. The devotion to their heritage and faith is seen in the manner in which the Greek families support their beloved St. Haralambos. September of 1961 marked the next milestone for the church community, as the mortgage was paid in full. That mortgage was a far cry from the estimates of what a new building would have cost.

After the move was completed, and St. Haralambos was sitting proud and beautiful on its new foundation at 25th Street and Harvard Avenue Northwest, it was estimated that 300,000 people had witnessed the move—not bad for a city of 100,000. The most excited of the viewers were these three gentlemen—George Michalos, John Kiminas, and Harry Paulos—who had risked their reputations as community leaders to move their beloved parish. They had an unshakable belief that God had called them to save the building which their fathers had constructed back in 1913.

Five

THE SPANISH COMMUNITY

Canton's Spanish community has always been a lively one. The first Spanish people came to Canton around 1914. Although there are no known pictures of them, we do know that the first Spaniards to arrive in Canton were: Antonio Cora, Bernardo and Lorenzo Vedodes, Manuel Castro, and Manny Sabaadra. It was not until 1917 that the first Spanish women came to Canton. Flora and Manual Perez are pictured here, shortly after their marriage. Flora was in the first wave of ladies who came to Canton from Cherry Bille, Kansas, in 1917, after the foundry in which she and other Spanish ladies worked was shut down.

Joaquina Ramos-Fernandez arrived in 1923, when a continuous influx of Spanish women were looking for Spanish men, in order to maintain a continuum of their strong Spanish culture. These women were, quite possibly, braver than the men, given the tenor of the times. Women were viewed as the "weaker gender," and apparently needed constant reminders that men were the stronger of the two sexes. There were no signs of weakness in these Spanish women, as they more than held their own in the Kansas foundries and the West Virginia glass factories.

Martina and Agosto Alarcon came to Canton from Brooklyn in the mid-1920s. In addition to managing the York Ice Company, Agosto and his wife, Martina, were dancers of some note. They are shown in authentic Argentine costumes dancing the tango, which they did in many public appearances around Canton.

Antonio Greene, grandson of Agosto and Martina, became a Spanish dancer of some note. He performed Flamenco dances around the Canton area for years. He is pictured here around 1960, after spending six months in Spain with Martina learning more of the culture, language, and dances.

Here, "Tony" is pictured in front of Tina's Confectionery on South Market Avenue, clowning with Grandma Tina. The confectionery had been the front yard of Tina's house. In 1945, she had this building put up to offer an ice cream and sandwich shop to the neighborhood.

The peak of the Alarcon family home can be seen in the background of this picture, which was taken the day Tina Alarcon had purchased a new car. The confectionery later became the Grenada Tavern, before it was finally razed in 1970 to make way for the new U.S. Route 30.

Toreadores, Picadores, and Guitaristas Ross, Greg, and Douglas Swank, are pictured in authentic Spanish bullfighter's attire, made especially for them by their grandmother, who spent many hours sewing over five thousand beads into them. It was a great deal of tedious work, but was simply one of those things that a true daughter of Spain would do to impress upon her grandsons just how important their heritage is, and to encourage them to remember the land of their forefathers.

The Spaniards brought their tradition of futbol with them to their adopted homeland. This is Victoria Aquero's photo of a team from 1927. Notice the snow on the ground and the players in their shorts. Even then it took tough people to play this international game. They played on vacant lots on Eighth Street Northeast, where Republic Steel later constructed a mill, which still stands today.

The Spanish people always loved a fiesta. In fact, they held one every year, with the first being in 1925. The public display of Spanish pride was very important to these early immigrants. They came at the tail end of the great immigration of the industrial age in America, and they had to work harder to gain the acceptance which earlier groups had already achieved. The earliest photo available of a fiesta is this one of the 1928 parade on Belden Avenue Northeast, which was where many of the Spanish immigrants lived.

In 1937, the fiesta featured these junior princesses: The girls, from left to right are: Margaret Sanchez-Conde, Louise Vega-Reed, and Anne Aquero-Fernandez. They are pictured in a lot in the northeast section of the city, which had the unseemly name of "Corn Center." Some people attribute this name to the number of illegal corn whiskey stills that operated there during Prohibition. It is also possible that there were many corn fields in that area in the early days of Canton's development. With the passage of time, the true reason for the name "Corn Center" has been lost to us.

Claudino Sanchez, the president of the Spanish Center (the support group before the building was constructed), is pictured here on the presidential float in the 1937 parade.

CORO JUVENIL DEL COMITE ANTIFACISTA ESPAÑOL DE CANTON, OHIO ~ U.S.A.

PHOTO BY FISHER

There were some difficulties in the Spanish community during the late 1930s, due to a very bitter strike at Republic Steel, where several men were killed by company guards, and due to the extremely divisive Spanish Civil War. The Loyalists (anti-Francisco Franco) were in the majority here in Canton, as these following pages illustrate. Several groups were organized to stage plays, hold dances, and perform choir concerts to raise money to support life in Spain as they remembered. The Fascists won the war, but not the hearts of these young ladies of the Anti-Fascist Youth Choir of Canton.

Emotions ran high among the anti-fascist Spaniards in Canton. In this picture from 1936, we see five young ladies. Pictured left to right are: Isabel Garcia, Augustina Peral-Perez, Josephine Monzu-Garrido, Bertha Rivera-Suarez, and an unknown young lady who is kneeling. They are posing in front of an ambulance which the Canton Anti-Fascist Committee for the Defense of Democracy of Spain planned to donate to the cause of the loyalist forces in the land of their birth.

The Spanish women were rabidly anti-fascist, and pictured here is the Grupo Feminino. This women's group was a broad-based gathering from across the entire Spanish community, and included several ladies who were not Spanish. The mother of Canton Art Museum Executive Director M.J. Albecete, who was Czechoslovakian, is in the top row on the far right.

Even though emotions ran high during 1936, the fiesta went on as usual. Here is the royal court: Queen Augustina Moran is in the center flanked by her princesses, Virginia Perez-Costa (right) and Isabel Mifsuit-Bandi (left). With no Spanish gathering place, many of the parades had the staging area in backyards of family homes near Belden Avenue Northeast. Isabel's father, Vicente, was the first president of the Spanish Center (before the building was constructed) and, tragically, he suffered a fatal heart attack during the Republic Steel strike of 1936.

This picture of the queen and her court is from the 1939 fiesta. The queen, Olga Garcia-Contrucci, is in the middle of the convertible. Flanking her on the right is Isabel Mifsuit-Bandi, and on the left is Frances Jiminez. It could never be said that judging for the royal court was based on anything other than the young ladies' ability to sell raffle tickets, for that was the only criteria for selection as queen or princess.

Pictured here, in the 1940 fiesta, is the maid of honor America Martinez-Gutierriez. Obviously her parents were proud, not only of her, but of this country which allowed them to enter and pursue their dream of a better life.

Here is the 1940 queen and her court: Frances Guerra-Rodriguez (center), America Martinez-Gutierriez (right), and Palmida Peral-Gonzalez (left). The queen and court were not chosen based on beauty, but on the basis of who sold the most raffle tickets.

The fiestas were part of the Spanish community, but the Spanish people lacked the one thing that bound the other ethnic groups together—a church. The Italians had St. Anthony's, the Irish had St. John's, and the Germans had St. Peter's, but there was no unifying parish which was predominantly Spanish in its origin. To address this shortcoming, a capital campaign was begun, and in 1941, the Spanish Center community building opened. Though it was not the largest building, it served the needs of the Spanish community for 50 years. As was the case for many other ethnic groups, the end of World War II led many of the returning veterans to move into the suburbs, where their children could have large yards in which to play and could breathe air untainted by mill smoke. Many people in the community loaned/donated money for the construction effort, and all were paid back in full.

The gathering clouds of a European war did not dim the fiesta in 1941. Perhaps it was because the Spanish community had already had a preview of the internal turmoil of conflict through their shared experience of the Spanish Civil War, or perhaps it was because the Spanish Center was now open for the community to showcase the progress that they had made in the 27 years since the intrepid six original Spanish men arrived. Frances Guerra-Rodriguez was the queen of the 1941 Spanish fiesta, and her expression is not one of a person fearful of the global crisis that was looming all around the community. The fiesta was a time to relax and have fun.

There were few
young men left
to participate in
athletic events
during the war,
so the Spanish
Center focused
on supporting the
war effort. After
the war, the center
sponsored several
athletic teams in the
community. Playing
for the Spanish
Center was very
important to these
young veterans.
They participated in
fast-pitch softball,
baseball, and the
ever popular futbol
(soccer), competing
against several other
ethnic teams.

The reputation of the Spanish fiesta spread, and in the post-war years the fiesta parade moved from Belden Avenue to downtown Canton. Making its way to the heart of Canton in 1948 is a float featuring guitaristas Francisco Guerra (in the white shirt) and Jose Blanco (his wife Mariquita is on the extreme left). The ladies on the right are Pearl Salcinas-Martin and Mary Genero.

That same parade saw some clowning around at the staging area, as Felipe and Angelo Sanchez pose with America Perez-Fernandez in front of a float near the Spanish Center.

Six

THE ITALIAN COMMUNITY

Quite possibly the most important Italian, albeit "honorary," was Canton educator Eva Sparrowgrove. She taught 48 years in the Canton system—first at Allen School and then at Timken High School. She not only taught many Italian students, but she also studied their language so she could communicate with the parents. If she heard of a sick mother, Eva would go to the home and cook for the family. Throughout World War II, Eva wrote to all of her "boys," and in some cases she made car and mortgage payments for them. Afterwards she also paid the college tuition for some of her outstanding students, who needed the assistance to make good with their lives.

While not sure of the exact year, this picture of Allen School's seventh and eighth grade classes features another of Canton's premiere educators. In the upper right-hand corner of the photograph is Lila Green. Lila's educational career has been capped with the honor of having the Black Educator's Association named for her. The BEA gives out scholarships annually to graduating seniors from Canton high schools.

Many Italian men left their homeland to find a better life in America. Biagio DioGuardi was no different. He left his native Greci, Italy, in 1913 to join his brother in the grocery business in Canton. He left his wife, Angelina, and infant son Michael, to live with his parents. They are shown in this 1916 picture, and in a pose that became a tradition, Momma Angelina stands with her hands on her hips. That was not a sign of anger, just her normal stance.

Biagio's older brother decided to return to Italy, and he sold the grocery store in 1919. Biagio bought the store and sent for his wife and son. DioGuardi's Italian Market became a mainstay at 745 Tenth Street Southeast. After getting the family settled in Canton, they began a lifelong affair with the grocery business. The family grew, and here Biagio posed with sons Michael and Victor. The younger DioGuardi son, Vic, went on to have a successful career in automobile sales.

The store lasted on Tenth Street Southeast until 1948, when Biagio moved it to its present location at 3116 Market Avenue North. He renamed it Heights Market, until fellow Italians accused him of selling out his heritage, and he put his name back on the store. Momma Angelina worked in the store every day making the "Best in the West" spaghetti sauce. Momma kept up with the business until she was 101 years old, always smiling and holding her hands on her hips. She sang Italian songs to keep everybody's spirits up. Angelina passed away at the age of 106.

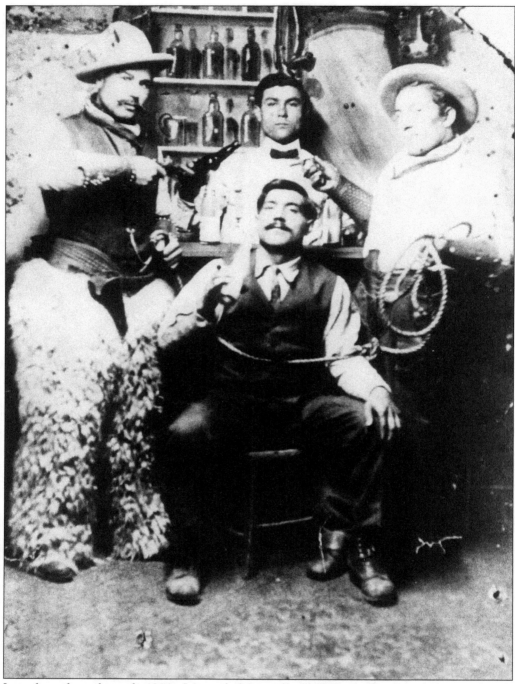

In a photo from the early 1920s, Leonardo Mazzarella (left), Biagio DioGuardi (center front), and Leonard Panella (right) pose as cowboys to help perpetuate the myth held by those left behind in Italy that America was all "cowboys and Indians." Many of these became the postcards that were sent back to Italy telling of the "wild times" that many immigrants were experiencing in their new homeland.

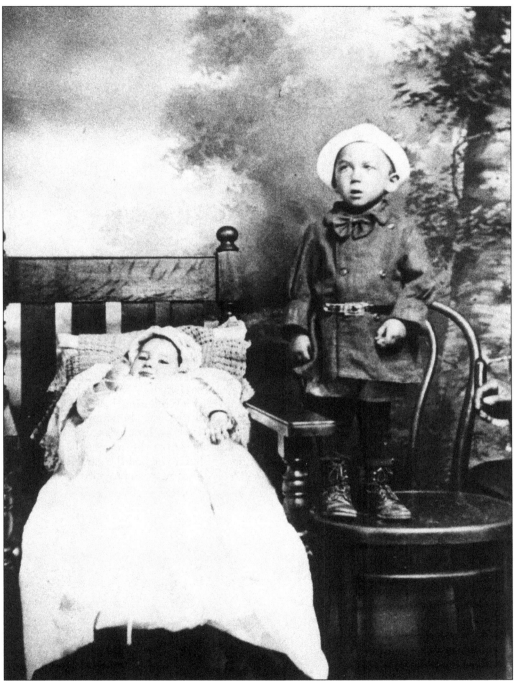

Leonardo Mazzarella's sons are pictured here in a 1916 photo. The "outdoor" backdrop was probably a canvas that the photographer carried. Many photographers made a business of traveling to the various communities in the area, as the cost of setting up a studio was prohibitive. Once he talked his way into the customer's home, he would pull out a few backdrops for the family to choose from for their special pictures.

This is the entire Mazzarella family: Momma Pasqualina (Panella), John, Ralph, and Papa Leonardo. Leonardo was a cement contractor and bricklayer during his working days in Canton. He and Pasqualina also had a huge garden, and they are also shown in this 1940s photograph. He was known by his neighbors as "Shorty Lee" for his garden work and sale of garden implements to the neighbors. The garden stretched from the rear of their home on Twelfth Street Southeast to Eleventh Street Southeast. Shorty Lee had the garden split in two sections, one for vegetables and the other for flowers. This huge garden provided food for many people during the Depression.

Leonardo was not a one-dimensional man. Each year he would don his costume and portray St. Bartolomeo for the annual Labor Day festival at St. Anthony's Church. Here he is at the 1911 festival, in full regalia. He had immigrated to America some years before, but always felt it his duty to make this portrayal of an "Old Country" icon, so that the tradition would not be lost on subsequent generations who had never experienced life in Italy.

The present-day location of the Salvation Army building was once the Robbins Furniture Store, and in 1919 it was on the route of a victory parade for returning World War I veterans. This float/decorated truck featured Leonardo Mazzarella's goat. Since his son Rep was allergic to cow's milk, Shorty Lee loaned out his goat for the parade. The William McKinley Sons of Italy Lodge (the name has been changed to the Ben Marconi Lodge) had its hall in the building as well.

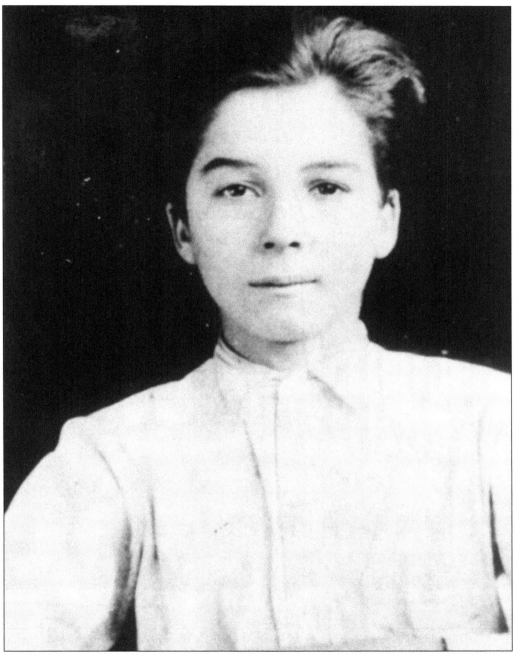

This is John Mazzarella at age 13, during the heyday of his *Repository* career. He looks no worse for wear after a childhood of drinking goat's milk. Day in and day out he stood on the corner of Cleveland Avenue and West Tuscarawas Streets hustling the paper. His nickname, Rep, came from the 15 years he stood on that corner hustling the *Canton Repository*. He took the first coin he made each day and carved the word "Rep" in the masonry of "his" building. When the building was about to be razed in the 1960s, an aging Rep had his daughter Marian take him to his corner to run his fingers over the letters one last time.

This is the building where "Rep" spent so much of his early life working. It was the old Central Savings Bank building. It is pictured here prior to the turn of the century, but one can imagine the young man etching the letters REP at ground level each day for 15 years. He was just marking his spot, so that no one else could horn in on his location. Over the years, many youths would fight to retain their corners. It was a matter of personal pride to be known by the downtown businessmen as "their" newsboy.

John "Rep" Mazzarella is shown in these photographs in front of Rep's Cycle Store. He is riding in a battery-operated car with his wife and is leaning on his storefront. Rep owned a bicycle and trailer rental store in the southwest of Canton. All those years as an independent "businessman" gave Rep an independence that he would not abandon in his adulthood. The bicycles he sold, and trailers he rented, made him a happy man.

Joseph Pileggi was born in Canton but moved to Brooklyn, New York, as a young man. He was involved in the grocery trade there, and when he visited family in Canton he always brought a fully stocked truck. In the 1960s, he moved back to his hometown. He is shown holding the helmet that his brother Armando wore the day he was killed fighting in Yugoslavia in 1920.

This is the Tortora family in a World War II family photo. The son, James, now sings and dances with the I Gagliardi Italiani troop, which strives to maintain much of the Italian culture for the city of Canton. This troop is very important to the Italian community, as many of the children of the original immigrants have married out of the Italian culture, and that dilution has led to a loss of some very fine traditions.

Oscar and Frances Lanzi are shown at an Italian-American Festival in Canton. Oscar owned a Sohio gasoline station in Canton, and for many years he held the exclusive towing contract with the Canton Police Department. The family was able to fulfill the contract after Oscar passed away, until the untimely death of his daughter Norma Schory, when the business was sold.

Seven

THE JEWISH COMMUNITY

As one of the early Jewish attorneys in Canton, Ernest Cohen had a most remarkable career. He graduated from McKinley High School in one of its first classes. Although he and his brother were orphaned due to the influenza epidemic of 1918, Ernie was not deterred. He graduated at age 16 and studied law at Baldwin Wallace College, completing his studies there by his 19th birthday. However, he could not take the bar exam, because at that time a prospective attorney had to be 21 years old. A waiver was needed from the State Supreme Court, and at age 19 Ernie argued his own case before the justices in Columbus. Chief Justice Carrington T. Marshall said that he would probably live to regret his decision, but Ernie was permitted to take the exam, and he passed. He is pictured here on a trip to Washington, D.C. in 1924. He was a rather striking young man and a great part of Jewish history in Canton.

People of the Jewish faith have been in Canton since the late 1860s, and they practiced their religion as they were able. It was not until the latter part of the nineteenth and early twentieth centuries that a great influx of Jews from Eastern Europe and Russia immigrated to this area. At that time, a more formalized Shul was necessary. This Shul (Temple), Agudas Achim, was located on Douglas Street (Ninth Street today), west of Cherry Southeast. It was dedicated in

Ruth and Ernie are pictured together here, in 1953, at the Jewish Welfare Fund Dinner. As parents of a Down Syndrome daughter, the Cohens have been at the forefront of care for the disabled and challenged citizens of our community. Ernie was one of the founders of the Stark County MRDD Board, having lobbied a state senator to introduce a bill, S. 169, which provides for the care and education of challenged Ohioans.

1913 with great solemnity, with a rather large crowd of the faithful in attendance. This was the temple for most of the Jewish families of Polish descent. One of the flags in the picture is of the Metro Club, made up of influential young men in the Jewish Community. The other flag, which is barely discernible, is the Star of David, and is always present in the Jewish community as a symbol of Jewish solidarity and faith.

Ernie Cohen's wife, Ruth, was as involved in the Canton community as her husband. She is pictured in these 1950s-era photographs at the annual Brandeis University luncheon, introducing George Alpert, the president of Brandeis, in April 1951.

This gentleman is Louis Hoicowitz, the epitome of the American success story. He was born in Vitebsk, the same town in which abstract-expressionist artist Marc Chagall was born. Hoicowitz immigrated to Canton to go into business with a friend. After a period of time, the partnership broke up, and Louis became a successful builder. He built Temple Israel on Twenty-Fifth Street and Harvard Avenue Northwest, and more than 12 homes in the toney Historic Ridgewood neighborhood in Canton. Two of his best homes are French Norman Revival style and are located at 2303 University Avenue Northwest and 132 Twenty-Second Street Northwest.

This is the Ritz apartment building, which Louis Hoicowitz built in the 1930s. It is still in remarkably good condition, a testament to the quality with which Mr. Hoicowitz operated his business. Louis was very involved in the Jewish community, working for the Jewish Center and the Temple Israel.

Louis and his wife Lottie (Barnett) are pictured here with their two daughters, Dorothy and Marilyn, in the backyard of their northwest section home in the late 1920s. Family was very important to Lou and Lottie. Lottie was a Cantonian by birth, and Louis had fled the pogroms to which Jews were summarily subjected in his native land. By all accounts, this was a family which had much to share with each other.

Eight

THE CATHOLIC FAITH

In 1817, Father Edward Fenwick said the first Mass under what has become famous as the Shorb oak tree, and from that rather inauspicious beginning sprang Canton's first Roman Catholic parish. Construction of the first church building began in 1823. It was during that construction that the man who did much to establish the Catholic faith in Canton, John Shorb, was killed by a falling timber. The remains of Mr. Shorb and his wife are buried in a common coffin along the west side of the church. This is a picture of the church building today. It has been called Domus Dei et porta coeli (House of God and gate of Heaven).

Nothing lasts forever, and that was true for the famous Shorb oak. The tree was struck by lightning in the early part of this century and died. Not wishing to lose contact with his heritage, an unknown craftsman carved the remains of the tree into this chair, which is still in use today.

This wooden Pieta, modeled after Michelangelo's marble piece in St. Peter's in Rome, hung over the main altar in the main arch. It is now located in the space which formerly housed the west confessional.

While St. John's has had an elementary school continuously since 1868, it was not until the fall of 1926 that this parish school enrolled Canton's first Catholic high school class. Construction had begun in 1925 on the building that still stands on church property. Classes were held in St. John's High School until the last class graduated in 1945. It then became the Boys Division of Central Catholic High School, in conjunction with the Mt. Marie Academy. Pictured here are some of the extra-curricular programs from St. John's: the 1926–27 boys' basketball team, the 1932–33 football team, the 1942–43 band, and the orchestra from the final year, 1945.

1932-33 Football Team

1926-27 Basketball Team

There have always been differences among peoples in this world, and that unfortunately extended to the immigrants who came to this country. By the middle of the nineteenth century, there was an influx of German-speaking peoples at St. John's, and they wanted Mass and confessions heard in their native language. In 1844, there was a split between the parishioners, and the new parish of St. Peter's was formed with the laying of the cornerstone in 1845. They are the only parishes in the diocese of Youngstown which share boundaries, and parishioners have free choice as to which they attend.

St. Peter's has had its school since 1860, and it gradually expanded to include ninth and tenth grades by 1883. Many students have passed through its building in the past 138 years, and we are fortunate to have access to some class pictures, provided by Winona Rossiter and Genevieve Moeglin, to remind us of the importance of Catholic education. We have this wonderful photograph of Mrs. Moeglin at her First Holy Communion in 1918, and as well as the entire class of Communicants from that year.

Genevieve Moeglin is one of the young ladies in these pictures of the 1920 fifth grade class and the 1924 eighth grade graduation class. Father Leo Schlindwein was the pastor during this time, and is remembered as being very kind to the schoolchildren. If some of the students look tired, it is because there were no school busses, and many of them had to walk long distances to receive their education. Father Schlindwein would often pick up and drop off some of the students who lived out in Waco.

Winona Rossiter is pictured in her First Holy Communion dress in 1924. We also have a darling photo of her mother, Elizabeth Kruk, in her 1901 First Holy Communion attire. Mrs. Rossiter's family has been affiliated with St. Peter's Church since 1889, when her grandparents were married there.

Mrs. Rossiter is pictured with her 1924 first grade class at St. Peter's, and also in her 1933 eighth grade graduation class picture. Winona is pictured in her first grade photograph in the top row near the center. She apparently wanted to make sure she remembered herself, as she has circled herself in the picture.

These three sisters were the beneficiaries of the kindness of the Sisters who taught at St. Peter's. We do not know who they are, but we do know that their First Communion dresses were made by the nuns. During the Great Depression, many families could not afford the traditional First Communion dresses for their daughters. So the nuns made dresses for each girl, and after the ceremony, the dresses were returned to the Sisters so they could be reused by the next group of communicants.

Nine

FOOTBALL AND RECREATION

Football has always been the name of the game in Stark County—especially the high school variety. As Stark County is the home of the Pro Football Hall of Fame, we must address the finest football player to ever don the uniform of the Canton Bulldogs—that would be this gentleman, Jim Thorpe. Jim came to Canton to play what passed for pro football in the post World War I era. Jim Thorpe has been called the greatest athlete of the first half of this century, and there are very few people who could argue the point. He came to play, and wound up as the president of the fledgling American Professional Football Association.

This rather imposing building at 205 Cleveland Avenue Southwest was the site of one of the most far-reaching events of the twentieth century on September 17, 1920. It was in the showroom of Ralph Hay's Hupmobile and Jordan automobile dealership that the National Football League was formed. Originally known as the American Professional Football Association, it had teams in such football hotbeds as: Canton, Cleveland, and Dayton in Ohio; Rochester in New York; Rock Island and Decatur in Illinois; Muncie and Hammond in Indiana; and Racine in Wisconsin.

CANTON BULLDOGS 1920
WORLD'S CHAMPIONS

ɟRIGGS, 2-BUCK, 3-O'CONNOR, 4-COCORAN, 5-MARTIN, 6-DADUM, 7-EDWARDS, 8-THORPE, 9-GUYON,
CALAC, II-HENRY, 12-GREEN, 13-WAHLEN, 14-GILROY, 15-SPECK, 16-FEENY, 17-HALEY, 18-HENDREN

In that inaugural season, the Canton Bulldogs emerged as champions, led by the immortal Jim Thorpe. Thorpe came to Canton from the Carlisle Indian School in Pennsylvania, and he brought three other Native Americans with him: Guyon, Pete Calac, and "Fats" Henry. All four became members of the Professional Football Hall Of Fame. Jim Thorpe also doubled as president of the league.

There was intense lobbying from the city of Canton to house the hall of fame here, and when the decision was made, this structure, known around the world, was built. Each summer since 1963, Cantonians and the world celebrate Football's Greatest Weekend at this shrine to gridiron greats. The "Weekend," over the years, has expanded to include a kickoff parade and hot air balloon fest the previous weekend, and a downtown ribs fest during the week in between. The feature game is played in this facility.

Fawcett Stadium was a WPA project constructed during the Great Depression. It has been a wonderful addition to the Canton City Schools Athletic Department, and there have been several hall-of-fame football players who started their careers on this field—the first of those being Marion Motley, a Cleveland Browns fullback in the Paul Brown era. P.B., as he was called by his associates and former players, only coached in this stadium on the years that Massillon Washington High played "the Game" at McKinley's home field.

VIEW MEYERS LAKE PARK, CANTON, OHIO

This is a summer's walk down the main concourse of Meyer's Lake Park. It was very relaxing and provided many days and nights of entertainment and relaxation to several generations of Cantonians. This walk is sorely missed.

Andrew Meyer was one of Canton's pioneers. He bought 3,000 acres from Canton's founder, Bezaleel Wells, and established a magnificent wheat farm, with a race track for his horses, along side a huge lake. After his death, the land became a campground owned by a brewery. During the time when Meyer's Lake was a relaxing area, there were cabins available for overnight stays. Each cabin had a name, so that visitors could request their favorite. Since Canton has virtually surrounded the lake, it seems odd to many of us that Meyer's Lake was once considered very rural. The land became an amusement park after the turn of the century, under the ownership of the Northern Ohio Light and Traction Company, but never a "big" park until George Sinclair bought it around 1926.

A local brewery was one of the first owners of Meyer's Lake after Andrew Meyer's death, and the picnic grounds and pavilions reflected this, as there is a keg mounted in a tree at the extreme right of the picture. Of course, the pavilions were built to save picnics from the scourge of ants, but wasps and hornets in the rafters were probably a little more problematic.

The Lake Side Street Car Company was one of several that provided transportation to the unbridled fun of Meyer's Lake recreation. At one time, the park was owned by the Northern Ohio Light and Traction Company. They provided social excursion rates to the park, bringing visitors from as far away as New Philadelphia and Cleveland. This hotel stood at Meyer's Lake for many years and offered a vacation for people from the far away cities that the Northern Ohio Light and Traction Company served.

There was once a wooden walkway across Meyer's Lake, and this family is enjoying their little trek—with the possible exception of the teenage daughter, who would probably rather be with her friends at that age. Perhaps she would have been more pleasant if she had been permitted to go swimming. Swimming was one of the most popular escapist activities during the long, hot summer months in the city. In the Victorian era, the bathhouse was a necessary evil. It allowed the properly modest Victorian lady to change into her long-sleeved bathing costume and not be seen until she entered the water. The young men of the era were also victims of the modest dress code. No self-respecting gentleman would ever appear in public with a bare chest. However, bare arms and legs, although somewhat risqué, were moderately tolerable.

This was the preferred manner for a gentlemen to court his lady on a warm, summer, Sunday afternoon. Canoeing on a lazy afternoon with one's sweetheart on the placid waters of Meyer's Lake was like achieving nirvana. It was also an innocent way to get your best girl away from younger siblings and nosy parents.

With the demise of the amusement park, fishing and boating have become the only recreational pursuit at Meyer's Lake. Here are several boats, awaiting their owners for a relaxing cruise across the placid waters. In the far right, there is an excursion boat similarly awaiting a call for a trip.

Now isn't that proper? Notice how everyone is so formally dressed for a day at Meyer's Lake. Talk of the merry-go-round, with its mechanical calliope, must have been all the rage at post-trip gatherings. The young ladies and children seem to be having fun, but it also seems that they are very grim-faced. Very few people smiled when their pictures were taken prior to 1940.

For the slightly older generation of our community, this is the Meyer's Lake we remember. Riding the Caterpillar or the Tilt-a-Whirl was enervating, exciting, scary (well, the first time anyway), and just plain fun! It seems such a shame that a virtual neighborhood playground could not have remained in our community, but some things must be relegated to our collective memories and cherished as a part of our Canton heritage.

As time progressed under the Sinclair family ownership, entertainment became the name of the game at Meyer's Lake. Here is the delightful Moonlight ballroom. It saw many of the twentieth century's biggest name bands and entertainers. Glenn Miller, Tommy Dorsey, Guy Lombardo, and others played here during its heyday. Unfortunately, it was on New Year's Day, 1979, that a spark from the annual New Year's Eve Gala caused a fire that totally destroyed the most enjoyable facility in the area.

Seen from an aerial view in the mid-1950s, Meyer's Lake was a full-blown amusement park, entertaining families and couples every summer. Progress, and the super parks like Cedar Point and Disney World, may have killed Meyer's Lake physically, but the memories of summer days and nights will live on in Cantonians' memories forever!